JAPANESE FRIED CHICKEN!

トリノカラアゲ!

BEING A BIRACIAL CHILD IN A MONORACIAL SOCIETY

単一民族の中に住むダブルルーツを持つ子供

H.L.B.III

This work contains actual events related to the author as truthfully as recollection permits and/or can be corroborated by research, with parts enhanced for literary purposes. Persons within are a mixture of actual individuals and composite characters. The names of all individuals have been changed to respect their privacy.

この作品は、筆者自身が見てきたこと、体験したことをもとに描かれました。描写をより表現力豊かにするために、多少話が付け加えられたところもあります。登場人物は、実在する人間とこの話のために造られた人物が共存しています。実在するすべての個人の名前は、プライバシーを尊重するために変更されました。

Helping ALL to see the innate and immeasurable value of each and every human life, starting with Japan and then to the World!

この世のすべての人が、自分の存在といのちの尊さを知ることができるように。日本から世界へ。

hopeforjapankatsudou@gmail.com

Dedication

This book is dedicated to all unique children everywhere.

このストーリーを、この世に生まれてきたすべてのユニークな子供たちに捧げる。

Foreword

“Japanese Fried Chicken!” Is an honest, child-like look at the challenges bi-racial children face in local schools in a mono-racial society, like Japan. It touches on the difficulties with which parents are also confronted in attempts to resolve such challenges.
It’s a small book with a big message.
—G.M. Bruce

まえがき

「みんなと同じがいい」を得意とする日本社会において、まわりと違う子どもたちは様々な困難に出くわす。
同時に、親たちもどのようにしてこの社会で子育てをしていくのかを考えなければならない。
短いストーリーだが、大きなメッセージが込められた本だ。
—G.M.ブルース

Acknowledgments

First and foremost: Tomomi Baker, my through-thick-and-thin forever partner, who, though we have four children together, unbegrudgingly allowed me to, for months, glue myself to our computer several hours daily. That she did so with love and patience and encouragement instead of bludgeoning me, burying my remains under our persimmon tree, and then pretending she had never been married to me at all is a testament to the fact that she is, in every sense of the term, my soulmate. As often as I can, I let her know how much I love and appreciate her. This is me informing the rest of the world, too.

There also are, of course, dozens of other people that I want to thank: my proofreaders, John Wilson, G.M. Bruce, Charles Moore, and Asha Boakye-Yiadom; illustration advisor, Lydia Kaylor; and my beta readers.

And I would be amiss to not thank my beautiful children. I came to this country mentally prepared for any challenge I would need to face; my children, on the other hand, had no choice. They are the most beautiful and innocent people on the face of the Earth. It breaks my heart to not be able to rescue them from the ignorance that exists in the world. That said, their candidness, openness, ability and willingness to share their day-to-day struggles and challenges, continue to fuel a passion in me to write!

And, also, great appreciation to the men of Life Church Japan who have committed to spiritually, mentally, and emotionally spur other men on to greatness; you all epitomize strong brotherhood and have the power to change the way men love and do life!

感謝の言葉

何よりもまず、私の永遠のパートナーであるトモミ・ベーカーに感謝をささげます。家に4人の子供が一緒にいながらも、何ヶ月もの間、毎日私が何時間もコンピューターの前に座ることを許してくれました。家の前にある柿の木の根元に、私の遺骨を埋めることもできたのでしょうが（笑）、そうはしませんでした。私のソウルメイトである妻に、毎日どれだけ彼女を愛しているか、感謝しているかを伝えます。今、このように書いていること、これがまさにそうです！

もちろん、他にも私が感謝したい人はたくさんいます。校正係のジョン・ウィルソン、G.M.ブルース、チャールズ・ムーア、アシャ・ボアキエ-ヤドム。イラストアドバイザーのリディア・ケイラー、私のベータ版の読者たち、そして日本語訳を手伝ってくれた友人たち。

次に、私の愛する子供たちへの感謝を忘れてはいけません。私はこの国に住み始めてから、直面してきたあるあらゆる課題に対し、精神的に備えることができました。一方で、私の子供たちは選択の余地はありませんでした。彼らは地球上で最も美しく純粋な存在です。この世の無知から彼らを救うことができないことは、私の心を痛めます。また、彼らの率直さ、オープンな心、能力、そして日々のちょっとした戦いや課題を共有してくれることによって、私自身の本を書くことへの情熱の刺激となっていることも事実です！

最後に、ライフチャーチジャパンの男性たちへ大きな感謝を捧げます。彼らは精神的、感情的にお互いを駆り立て、皆、強い友情を示してくれます。これらの素晴らしい男性たちは、人生を変える力を備えています！

"Tony, it's hot! Wait a minute!" exclaimed my mother.
I carefully put my book bag down quietly and skillfully tiptoed over to the kitchen table in my socks. I thought I was quieter than a ninja. But, my mother still turned around from the stove just as I was about to put a piece of freshly cooked chicken in my mouth.
How does she do that, I wondered!
My mother doesn't even have to turn around yet, somehow, she knows that I am there. Does your mother have this super-power too?
"I know that. I'll be ok," I said.
She raises her voice a lot, but I know she's not angry. I know this because she's raising her voice in English. When she raises her voice in Japanese, however, everybody listens; Japanese-speaking mothers mean what they say.

「トニー！まだ熱いからちょっと待って！」ママが大きな声で言った。
それはママが揚げていたからあげを、ちょうどぼくが一つ口に入れた瞬間のことだった。
そーっとランドセルを置いたぼくは、忍び足でキッチンテーブルへ向かった。きっと忍者よりも静かにやったぞ。それでもママにはお見通し。コンロに向かって、からあげをあげていたママがこっちを向いた時、ぼくは思わず思った。「なんでわかるんだ？！みんなのママもそう？」
「大丈夫だよ。熱いのは知ってたもん。」とぼくはママに答えた。
ママは大きな声をだす。でも今日のママはこわくない。だって今日は英語だったからさ。
ママが日本語で大きな声を出すときは一大事！日本語でしゃべるママはホントにこわい。
だから日本語でママが大声を出すときは、みんな言うことを聞くんだ。

I SEE YOU
見えてるわよ

"You all only listen to me when I raise my voice, huh?" my mother inquired. My mother doesn't raise her voice much on weekends. She does when we come home from school though.

I don't mean to upset her, but today she's making one of my favorite foods: Tori-No-Karaage. How could I resist? Tori-No-Karaage is Japanese-style fried chicken. There are never any bones, so it's very easy to eat. Tori-No-Karaage is always for lunch or dinner time; but today, my mother was frying some as an after-school snack. This is such an amazing way to come home!

Freshly fried Tori-No-Karaage is so good! You don't need any extra salt, ketchup, or anything.

Some kids wait until it cools down, but not me. I just use my superpower move, my Super-Monkey Wind-Breath, to cool the chicken down as I eat.

「みんなママが大声ださないと話を聞かないんだから！」
ママは週末にはあまり大声をださないけど、平日ぼくたちが学校から帰ると、よく大きな声を出す。今日も別にママに大声を出してほしいわけじゃなかったけど、
でも、今日はからあげを揚げていたんだもん。
ぼく、とりのからあげ大好き！骨がないから、食べやすい。
いつもはお昼ご飯か、夕ご飯にママは作るのに、今日はおやつの時間に揚げていたんだ。
揚げたてのからあげはサイコー！味はついているから、ケチャップも塩もいらない。
熱いから、冷めるまで待つ人もいるけど、ぼくはそうじゃない。ぼくのスーパーパワーだ！風(ふう)神(じん)猿(ざる)冷却(れいきゃく)！　これをつかって食べるんだ！

"Mom, so can I have some?" I asked.
"Go ahead Tony," Mother replied.
Here we go. Grab one, put it in your mouth and…ok, hoo hoo, oo oo!
I don't know why this works, but if you ever eat hot Tori-No-Karaage, try my Super-Monkey Wind-Breath superpower move. It really works!

「ねぇママ、ちょっと食べてもいい？」ママに聞いた。
「いいよ、トニー。」ママが言った。
やった！ひとつからあげを口に入れたら、ぼくのスーパーパワーで、フフフーの、フーフー！（サルのものまね）

"Tony," Mother said suddenly. I had already eaten three pieces.
"Yes," I answered, surprisingly.
"Please think about other people," she said. When she was talking to me she was looking right into my eyes and pulling the plate of Tori-No-Karaage away from me.
"I am, Mom. There are one, two, three, four, …twelve pieces of Tori-No-Karaage. Right?" I asked as I stopped her from moving the plate too far from me.

「トニー！」　急にママがまた大きな声を出した。
それはぼくがからあげを三つ食べたあとのことだった。
「はい！」とぼくはびっくりして答えた。
「ちゃんとほかの人のことも考えてね。」ママがまっすぐこっちを見ながら、
テーブルのからあげがのっているお皿をひっぱった。
「ママ、ぼくちゃんと考えているよ。見て。からあげは、いち、にぃ、さん、よん、、
１２こあるでしょ？」　ぼくは、からあげのお皿を少し引き寄せた。

“So that means that everyone can have three pieces,” I told her confidently.
“But there are six people, Tony.” Mother turned back to the stove to check the other Tori-No-Karaage that were still frying.
“What about Daddy and Mommy?” she asked in Japanese while tapping her foot.
“Oh. You want some too?” I asked.

「ひとり３こずつってことでしょ？」ぼくは胸を張って答えた。
「でもトニー、うちは６人家族でしょう？」　ママがもう一度コンロに戻って、
残りのからあげを数えた。
「パパとママは？食べないっていうの？」　ママが日本語で聞いてきた。
ママは腕を組みながら右足のつま先を床にトントンしていた。
「え？ママたちも食べるの？」　ぼくは聞いた。

12÷4=3
12 PIECES OF KARAAGE
から揚げ12個
4 KIDS
子供4人

I'm Japanese, but I don't look Japanese.
Are you confused yet? Ha ha!
Can you find me? Look very carefully.
No, not that boy. I'm in the upper-left corner.
Yup, that's me.
I'm Japanese. I'm also African-American.
I'm in the second grade. I like to play soccer, tag, and I like to draw with my friends.

ぼくは日本人だけど、日本人に見えない。
ぼくの言っていること、わかる？　フフフ
ぼくを探してみて！よーく見てね。
ちがうよー。ぼくは左上にいるよ。
そう、それがぼく。
ぼくには、日本人とアフリカ系アメリカ人の血が流れている。
ぼくは小学二年生。サッカーとおにごっこが好き。
あと、友だちと一緒に絵を描くことも好き。

TONY DOESN'T LIKE MATH BUT HIS FRIEND HANA, DOES. トニーは算数がきらいだけど、友だちのはなちゃんは算数好き

Going to school is fun because I can play with my friends - but I don't like math. Most of my friends don't like math, either. My brother doesn't like math. And more importantly, I can't play video games if I don't do well in 'all' of my classes. So my math grades are always good, but I still don't like math. Do I know anyone who 'likes' math?

ぼくは学校が好き。友だちと一緒に遊べるから。あ、でも算数は嫌い。
ぼくの友だちも算数は嫌い。ぼくのお兄ちゃんも算数は嫌い。
でもぼく、全部の授業でがんばらないとテレビゲームができないんだ。
だから、算数もがんばる。
でもやっぱり、算数は嫌い。算数が好きな人っているのかなぁ。

When Tomoka was 14, she had 14 candles on her birthday cake. 5 girls came to her birthday party that year. They each brought 2 gifts. This year, Tomoka had 6 more candles on her birthday cake and 6 girls came to her party.
4 girls brought 2 gifts and 2 girls brought 3 gifts.
How old is Tomoka now? How many gifts did she receive?

$$14 + 6 = 20$$

$$4 \times 2 = 8$$

$$2 \times 3 = 6$$

Oh yeah! My friend Hana-chan likes math. Hana-chan sits next to me in class. When we have to do math worksheets, she looks down, and her hair covers the desk like an umbrella. Then she throws her head back like she's about to take a picture. She doesn't use her fingers to add or subtract like I sometimes do; she nods left-to-right and up-and-down like she's counting with her nose. Then she smiles when she has the answer and throws her head and all of her hair down again. My hair doesn't move at all, so no umbrella hair for me.

あ！そういえば、はなちゃんは算数が好きだって言っていた！はなちゃんは、ぼくのとなりに座っている女の子。算数プリントをやっているとき、はなちゃんはかみの毛でプリントをおおってしまう。傘みたいに！それからカメラでポーズをとる時みたいに、かみの毛を後ろにサッと振るんだ。はなちゃんは、ぼくみたいに足し算や引き算の時には指を使わない。少し顔を傾けたり、上を向いたり下を向いたりしている。まるで、鼻でも使って数えているみたいに。答えが合っているとわかった時は、にこっと笑って、またかみの毛の傘を、机でうつむきながら開く。ぼくのかみの毛はほとんど動かないから、かみの傘はできないな。

Anyway, after lunch, my friends and I always play together at recess.
So, one day I was playing tag with my friends Junya-kun and Takuto-kun. Playing tag in the summer is so much fun. There aren't many trees in the middle of the school yard, so my hat keeps the sun and sweat out of my eyes.
I can run super - super fast. Takuto-kun is fast too, but not Junya-kun.
One day, I was 'It' ; so, I tried to make myself run even faster. Faster! Faster!! I might be running as fast a bullet train! Takuto-kun was right behind me.

"Oops! My Hat!!"

The wind pushed up on the bill of my hat and it flew off.

そんなことはさておき、ぼくはいつもお昼休みに友だちと一緒に遊ぶ。
ある日、ぼくとじゅんや君、たくと君でおにごっこをして遊んでいた。夏の暑い日は、
ぼくの帽子が大活躍。日よけにもなるし、汗が顔に垂れてこないから助かる。
ぼくは走るのが得意。たくと君も速い。でも、じゅんや君は遅い。
ぼくがおにだったから、めちゃくちゃ速く走った。もっと速く！もっと速く！
新幹線みたいにがんばったんだから。たくと君はぼくのすぐ後ろを走っていた。
「あー！帽子が！」　ぼくの帽子が！！
帽子が風で飛ばされた！

No! No! No!
あかん!

In class, I don't wear my hat; but I do wear it in the hallways and at recess.
I don't want to wear my hat because it pushes my hair down and then I have to comb it out again. Combing really hurts! My dad taught me to comb it when I come out of the shower. I don't understand why this helps, but it doesn't hurt as much when my hair is wet. It's like magic! It still hurts a lot to comb it when it's dry, but I don't cry much anymore. Sometimes, I hate my hair!

授業中はかぶらないけど、廊下にいる時と、休憩時間に、ぼくは帽子をかぶる。かぶりたくないんだけどね。ぼくが帽子をかぶると、かみの毛が押されて、またかみをくしでとかさなきゃいけなくなるから。くしを通すのは本当に痛い。パパが、お風呂からあがってからすぐにくしを通すといいと教えてくれた。なんでかわからないけど、かみの毛がぬれていると、くしを通しても、そこまで痛くないんだ。魔法でもかかったみたいに！　乾いているときはすごく痛い。でも、もうそれでも泣かなくなったけどね。ときどき、ぼくは自分の髪がきらいだ！

My dad asked my mom to buy me a sun visor. She found this awesome one that is reversible: one side is red and the other side is white. My sun visor is so cool. When I go out with my family, I use my sun visor - but I don't wear it to school anymore. I use a hat that covers my hair now.
I thought everyone was going to think my sun visor was cool too, but some of the six-graders didn't think it was cool at all. Some of the six-graders are mean; they always point, laugh and say negative things about me and my hair. Some of the boys used to push me too. They always try to bother me. I don't let it hurt me though, because they always say the same silly things. They are not 'my' friends. At least we are not in the same class. And my mom said,

"Don't worry Tony. They are going to graduate and leave soon."

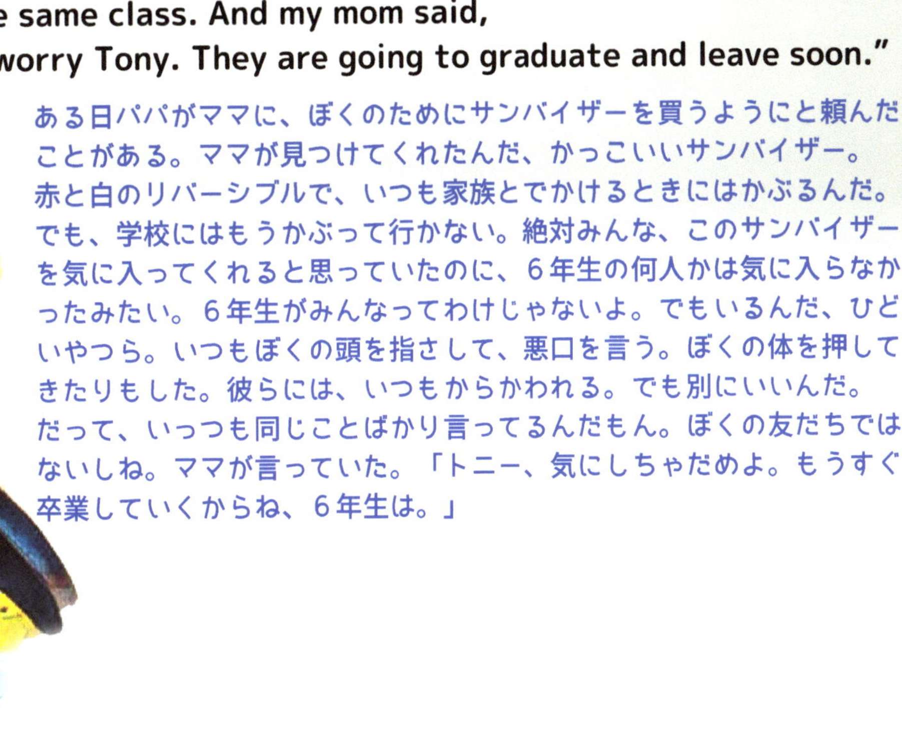

ある日パパがママに、ぼくのためにサンバイザーを買うようにと頼んだことがある。ママが見つけてくれたんだ、かっこいいサンバイザー。赤と白のリバーシブルで、いつも家族とでかけるときにはかぶるんだ。でも、学校にはもうかぶって行かない。絶対みんな、このサンバイザーを気に入ってくれると思っていたのに、６年生の何人かは気に入らなかったみたい。６年生がみんなってわけじゃないよ。でもいるんだ、ひどいやつら。いつもぼくの頭を指さして、悪口を言う。ぼくの体を押してきたりもした。彼らには、いつもからかわれる。でも別にいいんだ。だって、いっつも同じことばかり言ってるんだもん。ぼくの友だちではないしね。ママが言っていた。「トニー、気にしちゃだめよ。もうすぐ卒業していくからね、６年生は。」

Stupid wind, I thought.
"Ha ha! Tori-No-Karaage," Junya screamed as he pointed at my hair.

「風のやつめ！」とぼくは思った。
「アハハ！とりのからあげだ！」じゅんや君が、ぼくの髪の毛を指さしながら叫んだ。

TONY'S FRIEND, JUNYA トニーの友だちのじゅんや君

Junya doesn't always listen. He likes to wear shirts with cheetahs or other big cats. And he likes to wear black pants. When we're in the classroom, he doesn't always do what the teacher says. Sometimes, he pushes his books on the floor on purpose and everybody looks at him. I know I'm not supposed to laugh, but it makes me laugh. No, wait! It's not funny 'all' the time.
Sometimes I can't hear the teacher. That's really not good because I want to do well in all of my classes. Junya doesn't know that I can't play video games if I get bad grades.
So, I ask him to stop a lot. He listens when I ask him, so I always forgive him, and then we play together again.

じゅんや君は悪ガキだ。いつもチーターやトラの絵のシャツを着ている。
ズボンはいつも黒。授業中も、先生の言うことを聞かない。みんなの注目をあびたいから、
わざと教科書を床に落としたりする。笑っちゃいけないとわかっているけど、おもしろい。
あれ？おもしろくないか！
だって、先生の言うことは聞こえないし、そしたらテストでも良い点が取れない。
そしたら、ぼくはゲームができなくなる！！
でも、じゅんや君はぼくのゲームのことなんかは知らない。
だから、ぼくはよくじゅんや君に、「やめて」と言う。じゅんや君はぼくの言うことを
聞いてくれるから、ぼくはいつも彼をゆるしてあげられる。そしてまた一緒に遊ぶ。
いつも、これのくり返しだ。

"Yeah! It looks like burnt Tori-No-Karaage," agreed Takuto.
Takuto has been my friend since kindergarten. We play a lot together. Takuto looks like a big kid. Well, he's not as tall as me, but he has an older-looking 'daddy face': his eyebrows are thick and he already has a mustache!
He has seen my hair many times before, and has never said negative things. I really wish they hadn't said that about my hair.

「ほんとだ！焦げたとりのからあげみたい！」たくと君も言った。
たくと君とぼくは、幼稚園からのお友だち。いつも一緒に遊ぶ。たくと君は、おとなみたいな子ども。背はぼくより少しだけ低い。でも、顔がもうオヤジみたいなんだ。まゆ毛も太いし、なんだか口ひげも生えているみたい。たくと君は、今までぼくのかみの毛のことで、悪口は何も言ったことがなかったのに。
ぼくは友だちが、ぼくのかみの毛のことでいろいろ言う時、すごくいやなきもちになる。

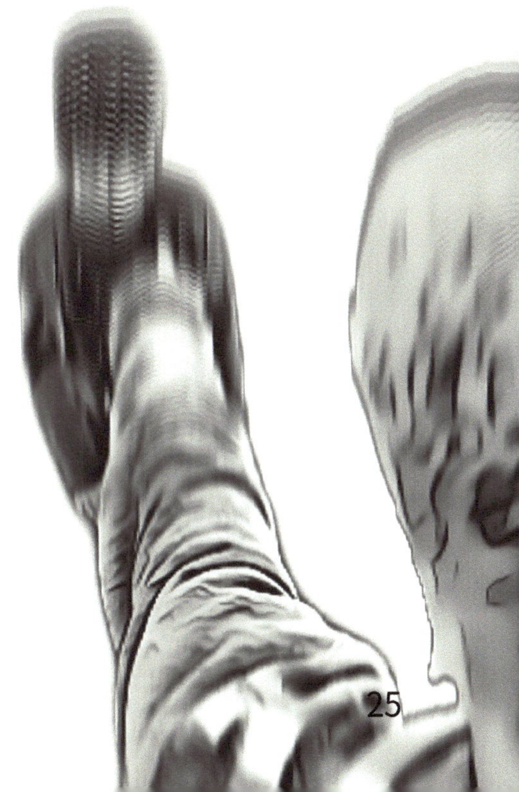

Just don't look at them, I thought.
"Don't you dare cry Tony!" I loudly whispered to myself.
Oh, no! One tear fell.
I picked up my hat, and secretly wiped the tear as I put it back on, and kept playing. I didn't really want to play anymore, but I didn't want my friends to know that I was sad, either.

ふたりから目を離そう、とふと思った。
「ここで泣いちゃだめだぞ！」ぼくは自分の心の中で言った。
あ！だめだ！涙がこぼれてきた。
ぼくは、地面に落ちていた帽子をひろって、周りにわからないように、
涙をそでてでぬぐった。帽子をかぶってから、彼らとまた遊んだ。
ほんとは遊びたくなかったけど、ぼくが悲しんでいたことを、
ふたりに知られたくなかったんだ。

Hurry and wipe your tear!
はやく涙拭かなきゃ！

If I had straight hair, maybe they wouldn't have laughed at me, I wondered.
It was hard to keep smiling at school that day. In my head I kept hearing, "*Tori-No-Karaage.*" I thought I was going to scream at my friends, or even hit them. I felt so hurt and angry. But then, I heard my dad's voice in my head:
"Say it Tony," he said.

もしぼくのかみの毛が、まっすぐだったら、笑わなかったかなぁ。
その日は、学校でもずっと悲しい気持ちが続いた。頭の中で、「とりのからあげ」がぐるぐる回っていた。
ぼくは、友だちにどなり返すか、なぐってやろうかと思った。でもその時に、頭の中でパパの声が聞こえた。
「トニー、言ってみなさい。」とパパが言った。

I am unique.
No one can duplicate anything I can do, nor will I let anyone define who I am.
My brother, sisters, and I have to say this every morning and night to remind ourselves that we are unique and special.
My dad's voice came into my head. I don't know why, but I am glad that I could finish school that day.

ぼくはユニークに造られた。
ぼくがすることは、ほかの人がまねしても同じようにはできない。ほかの人がぼくのことをどう呼ぼうと、ぼくはぼくでいい。
ぼくにはお兄ちゃんと、妹が二人いるけど、毎朝毎晩この言葉を宣言する。
パパの声が、そう頭の中で聞こえてからは、その日はなんとか学校にいることができた。

School finished. I went home and started doing my homework.
I wasn't going to tell my mom what happened, but then she started frying Tori-No-Karaage!
Suddenly, I couldn't see! My eyeballs were swimming in tears.
I told my mom everything that had happened. She hugged me and then dried my face with her sleeve. She told my dad when he came home from work.

ぼくは学校が終わって、家に帰り、そして宿題をやり始めた。その日学校で起きたことを、
ママには言うつもりはなかった。でも、ママがとりのからあげを揚げ始めた！
急に目が見えなくなった。涙があふれすぎて。
ママに、学校で何が起きたかを話した。ママはぼくをハグして、涙をそでで拭いてくれた。
ママは、パパが家に戻ってきてから、パパにぼくのことを話した。

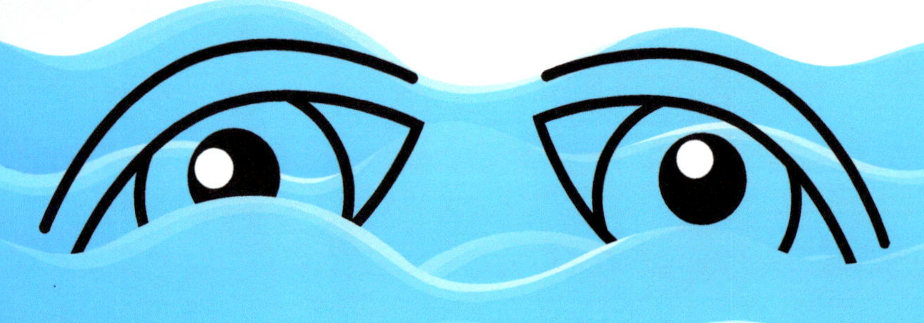

My dad told me again how special I am. Then he asked me the question that he always asks:

"How does Daddy love you?"

"With all your heart. No matter what. For now, and forever," I said.

"That's right Tony," he said.

"Do you want me to go to your school and talk to your friends?" he asked.

パパはぼくに、ぼくがどれだけ特別な存在であるかを言ってくれた。そして、いつもの質問をぼくにした。

「パパはトニーのことをどんなふうに愛してる？」

「いつまでも、何があっても、心を尽くして愛してくれる。」　ぼくが答えた。

「そうだね、トニー。」パパが言った。

「パパが学校の友だちに話しに行ったほうがいいかい？」パパが聞いてきた。

I remember when he went to the house of a boy who was bothering my older brother. The boy was pushing my brother at school every day. Sometimes, he would push my brother so hard that he would fall down and he would get hurt. When my brother told Dad, I remember my dad became visibly upset. He looked at my brother and I and said:

"I'm not angry at you, I'm angry that you have to deal with such treatment. I am always on your side." He was sitting on the other side of the dining room table, so I didn't understand why he said, "I'm on your side."

My brother was so happy and the boy ended up feeling so sorry and was afraid to bully my brother ever again. So, I know my dad would really come to help if I needed him.

"No. Let's write to the teacher and see what happens first," I said.

お兄ちゃんが、一年生の時に、ある友だちにからかわれていたのを思い出した。その子は、
お兄ちゃんを毎日押して、ちょっかいを出した。時には、強く押されてお兄ちゃんが地面に
たたきつけられて、けがをしたこともある。お兄ちゃんがそのことをパパに話したら、
パパはものすごく怒ったんだ。パパは、お兄ちゃんとぼくを見て、こう言った。
「パパは君たちに対して怒っているんじゃないんだ。君たちと一緒に怒っているんだ。
パパはいつも君たちと同じ側に立っているんだ。（君たちの味方だ）」
パパは、ぼくらとはテーブルの反対側に座っていたから、なんで「同じ側に立っている」って
言ったかは、その時ぼくはよくわからなかった。お兄ちゃんはその後、その子がもう謝って、
からかうのもやめたから、嬉しそうだった。
パパは、必要だったらぼくにも同じようにやってくれると、ぼくは信じていた。
「まずは連絡帳で先生にきいてみたい。」ぼくが言った。

My mom wrote to my teacher and my teacher talked to my friends and classmates the same day! Then, she also called their moms! I don't know what their moms said, but I could tell that my friends and classmates were really sorry. They don't say negative things about my hair anymore. I think now they just see unique Tony.

ママが連絡帳で先生に書いてから、その日中に保護者たちにも電話で話してくれた。
たくと君とじゅんや君のママが何を言ったかは、ぼくは知らないけど、二人とも
謝ってくれた。そして、もうぼくの髪の毛のことでは何も言わなくなった。
ぼくのユニークさとして、今は見てくれているのかな。

Oh! Maybe I should teach them my *Super-Monkey Wind-Breath* superpower move!

"Mom!"

"Yes, Tony?"

"Can my friends come over for dinner?"

"And can you please make Tori-No-Karaage?"

あ！そういえば、じゅんや君とたくと君に、
僕のスペシャルパワーの風神猿冷却をまだ教えていなかった！

「ママ、」

「何？トニー？」

「友だちを夕食に誘ってもいい？」

「からあげを作ってほしいんだけど。」

PRONUNCIATION GUIDE

Tori-no-karaage	toh-ree noh kah-rah-ah-gay
Junya-kun	joon-yaa koon
Takuto-kun	tah-koo-toh koon
Hana-chan	hah-nah chahn

CULTURAL NOTE

Japanese people usually call each other by their family name rather than their given names. An honorific is almost always attached to the name. The most common, gender neutral 'San', could be translated as "Mr.", "Mrs." and "Ms.". The informal 'Kun', is strictly reserved to young men or juniors. 'Kun' is used by a person of a higher status towards a younger male or a child. Friends can also refer to each other by 'Kun' in a casual context and women can use it to address a man to whom they are very close. 'Chan' refers to children and girls. Changing "s" sound to "ch" is considered soft and cute in Japanese. It is used to refer to young women you are close with, children, babies, a grandmother or even a favorite animal friend. Just like the honorific 'Kun', friends and lovers can also address each other with this suffix.

Karaage is widely available in festivals and food stalls throughout Japan. It has been a popular food since the 1920s. Karaage generally refers to fried chicken, but there are also fish, beef, and pork variations. Each region in Japan has their own version of this family favorite.

www.ingramcontent.com/pod-product-compliance
Ingram Content Group UK Ltd.
Pitfield, Milton Keynes, MK11 3LW, UK
UKHW060113300726
14090UKWH00002B/160

9798502853958